Swamp wattle

Acacia oncinocarpa

Family name: FABACEAE (pea family)

Summary: Flooding the mid layer of savannah woodlands in a profusion of yellow, this shrub's flowers signal the onset of the dry season. These plants are a fast-growing and reasonably short-lived species that are useful for rehabilitation work or screening purposes in streetscapes.

Description: A tall, spreading shrub to 4 m. The bark is dark grey and fissured. The grey-green phyllodes are either straight or curved with 3 prominent primary veins. These are widest in the middle and are 5–11 cm long by 1–3 cm wide. The flowers are pale yellow spikes from 3–8 cm long and are clustered towards the end of branches. The fruit are erect, brown, oblong woody pods up to 11 cm long by 1 cm wide. These have slightly obscured diagonal venation and thickened margins with a prominent hooked tip. At maturity the pods split to release the black seeds that are diagonally placed inside them.

Flowering time: March to August.

Habitat: Common in open forests or woodlands on lateritic soils. The species can grow vigorously on exposed or disturbed sites. Also found in sandstone country.

Distribution: Widespread across the Top End and extending into the Kimberley.

Origin of name: 'oncinocarpa', Greek *ogcinos* hook, and *carpos* fruit, in reference to the small hook found at the top of the pods.

Wattle

Alstonia actinophylla

Family name: APOCYNACEAE (periwinkle family)

Summary: A large, stately tree, often with a gnarled trunk and twisting branches. The older and larger trees have a commanding presence in open woodlands where their distinctive form stands out. The common name is derived from the milky sap.

Description: A tall, spreading tree to 20 m. The bark is cream to pale grey, thick and corky. The leaves are whorled with 4–7 leaves per whorl. These are narrow and lanceolate in shape, 5–10 cm long by 1–3 cm wide. The leaves are light green above and paler on the underside. The small, white, star-shaped flowers are densely clustered on long stalks at the end of branches. The fruit are paired, long, narrow, papery pods that split when ripe, revealing small, flat seeds with silky hairs.

Flowering time: August to October.

Habitat: Grows in open forests and woodlands, coastal vine thickets, margins of coastal floodplains, rocky outcrops in monsoon vine thickets and cliff tops. Generally found on well-drained sites or in transition zones margining drainage areas.

Distribution: Scattered across the Top End and extending into Western Australia and Queensland.

Origin of name: 'Alstonia', after Charles Alston (1685–1760), a Scottish physician and professor of botany at Edinburgh (1716–1760); 'actinophylla', Greek *actis* ray, spoke of a wheel, and *phyllon* leaf, in reference to the leaf arrangement being whorled.

Milkwood

Ampelocissus frutescens

Family name: VITACEAE (grape family)

Summary: The grape-like fruit on this shrub packs a punch. At first sweet, it is followed by a spicy aftertaste rather like a bad shiraz. It is a distinctive shrub, standing tall with grape-like leaves and clusters of dark purple to black fruit.

Description: An erect shrub to 1.5 m, produced annually from a perennial tuber. The leaves are compound with 3–7 but mostly 5 leaflets. These are coarse, obovate in shape (broadest at the tip) and often have tangled long hairs. The flowers are small, purple and clustered towards the end of branches. These develop into clusters of fleshy, oval fruit, 1–1.2 cm long by 0.5–0.8 cm wide that mature to a dark purple-black. Each grape contains two seeds.

Flowering time: February to May.

Habitat: A widespread species in open forests and woodlands on a variety of geology and soil types. Usually found on plains and gentle rises, commonly on gravelly soils.

Distribution: Common in the Top End and extending into parts of the Kimberley and northern Queensland.

Origin of name: 'Ampelocissus', Greek *ampelos* vine, and *cissos* ivy, in reference to the grape-like appearance of this species; 'frutescens', Latin *frutex* shrub, bush, in reference to the habit of this plant.

Wild grape

Banksia dentata

Family name: PROTEACEAE (grevillea family)

Summary: The Territory's only *Banksia* species, this plant evokes images of the big bad banksia men from the Snugglepot and Cuddlepie stories written by May Gibbs in 1946. However, these gorgeous and distinct trees soften their surrounds with their holly-shaped foliage and beautiful protea-like flowers.

Description: A shrub or small, spreading tree to 6 m. The bark is rough and dark grey. The holly-shaped leaves are distinct and long with a glossy dark green surface and white underside. They are alternate, have a prominent mid-vein and range from 14–27 cm long by 5–7 cm wide. The flowers are large, dense, yellow spikes to 13 cm long by 10 cm wide. The fruit are formed within the rough woody cylindrical cone. These open when ripe to reveal two hard woody valves that contain two wedge-shaped, winged black seeds.

Flowering time: March to August.

Habitat: Freshwater creek banks, swamps and drainage depressions, commonly on seasonally inundated sandy soils.

Distribution: Common around the northern-most parts of the Top End and other parts of northern Australia and New Guinea.

Origin of name: 'Banksia', for Sir Joseph Banks (1743–1820), who sailed with Captain Cook, collected the largest private herbarium in Europe and was a leading patron of the natural sciences; 'dentata', Latin *dentata,* toothed, in reference to the leaves' margins.

Swamp banksia

Barringtonia acutangula

Family name: LECYTHIDACEAE (brazil nut family)

Summary: Lining creeks and rivers, the freshwater mangrove is found along most of the well-known fishing spots in the Top End. Used by Aboriginal people as a fish poison, the bark is crushed and placed in waterholes and the intoxicated fish are forced to the surface where they are easily gathered. The trees are also home to caterpillars that can cause severe irritation if touched.

Description: A small to medium multi-stemmed and spreading tree to 8 m. The bark is dark grey, rough and fissured. The leaves are alternate and usually crowded towards the end of branches, light green and elliptic in shape (tapered towards each end), with finely serrated margins, 6–15 cm long by 2–5 cm wide. The flowers are red sprays that hang down on long, pendulous stalks up to 20 cm long. The fruit are 3–6 cm long, roughly oval-shaped with four distinctive ridges or corners. These encase a single seed.

Flowering time: Periodic, but usually July to September.

Habitat: Along freshwater creeks, rivers, billabongs and swamps on clay soils.

Distribution: Widespread across northern Australia.

Origin of name: 'Barringtonia' after Daines Barrington (1710–1800), an English botanist; 'acutangular', Latin *acutus* sharp pointed, and *angulus* angle, in reference to the four-cornered fruit.

Freshwater mangrove

Brachychiton megaphyllus

Family name: MALVACEAE (hibiscus family)

Summary: This is the floral emblem for the city of Darwin. The species flowers once its leaves have dropped, and this is the time that the tree catches your eye. The striking red flowers are plastered along bare grey branches. Later follow the pods, equally memorable, like small boat-shaped vessels.

Description: A small, deciduous tree to 6 m. The bark is dark grey-brown, slightly fissured and tessellated. The leaves are alternate, large and almost circular, 15–26 cm long by 10–22 cm wide, with up to 3 lobes. The leaf base is distinctly heart-shaped and the leaves are softly hairy and are usually largest when young. The bell-shaped flowers are up to 4 cm long and are orange-red with 5 petals. These are clustered towards the end of branches. The fruit are large, woody oblong vessels, covered with short yellow-brown bristly hairs and split when mature. The fruit contain numerous small, yellow seeds encased in thick bristly hairs.

Flowering time: June to October.

Habitat: An understorey plant in eucalypt open forests and woodlands. The species is generally found on deep red and brown earths of a lateritic origin or on shallower granitic soils.

Distribution: Widespread north of Katherine, including the immediate Katherine area.

Origin of name: 'Brachychiton', Greek *brachys* short, and *chiton* tunic, in reference to the seeds having a hairy outer coat; 'megaphyllus', Greek *megas* great, and *phyllon* meaning leaf, in reference to the size of the adult and juvenile leaves.

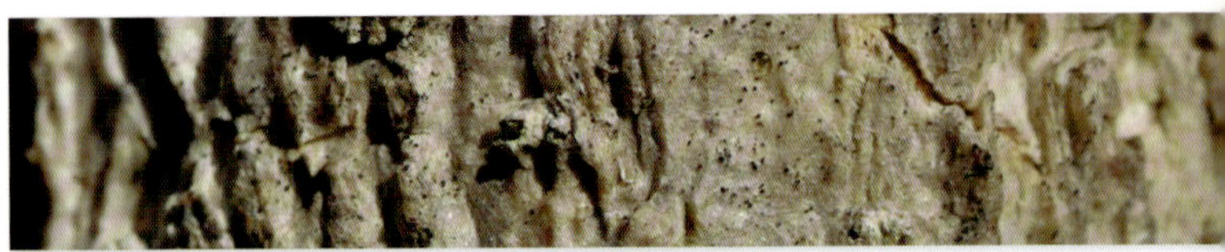

Red-flowering kurrajong

Buchanania obovata

Family name: ANACARDIACEAE (cashew family)

Summary: Related to the commercial mango, this species has small, mango-shaped fruit that are tart and tangy. These trees are valued by Aboriginal people for a myriad of uses in addition to the edible fruit: the wood is used to make woomeras and the bark is boiled to make dye or used as a fish poison.

Description: A small and often untidy tree to 10 m. The bark is grey and usually rough and tessellated. The leaves are thick and leathery, wider above the middle and taper at the base, ranging from 10–25 cm long by 3–10 cm wide. The leaves have distinct lateral venation and a raised mid-rib. The flowers are small, cream and are borne on long, slender stalks growing from the end of branches. The oval fruit are fleshy, and mature to a light green when ripe. These are up to 1.5 cm long and encase a single seed.

Flowering time: July to October.

Habitat: A widespread species in open forests and woodlands on a variety of well-drained soils.

Distribution: Common in the Top End and Victoria River District extending to the Kimberley and Queensland.

Origin of name: 'Buchanania' after Francis Buchanan-Hamilton (1762–1829), superintendent of the Calcutta Botanical Gardens; 'obovata', Latin *ob* inverted, and *ovatus* egg-shaped, in reference to the leaves being broadest above the middle.

Green plum

Calytrix exstipulata

Summary: Southern states have their yellow and red autumn displays, but this pink spectacular is our Top End equivalent. Turkey bush is unforgettable in full flower. It is a hardy species, but proves difficult to grow at home in a nurtured environment.

Description: A tall, upright shrub to 3 m. The tiny leaves are densely packed and almost overlap on stems and small branches (heath-like). The bark is grey and rough. The flowers are star-shaped with prominent stamens and are clustered towards the end of branches. The flowers are up to 2.5 cm long by 2.5 cm wide, ranging from pink to magenta. The fruit is a small nut-like seed that remains inside the flower tube; as the flowers dry and fall to the ground, the seed is spread.

Flowering time: May to August.

Habitat: A widespread species common in disturbed areas in shallow lateritic soils or sandstone areas. It grows in a range of habitats from skeletal slopes to open plains and commonly colonises roadside verges and gravel pits.

Distribution: Widespread from the Top End to the Kimberley.

Origin of name: 'Calytrix' from greek *calyx* meaning cup, in reference to the flower, and *thrix*, *trichos* refering to the long, stiff hairs coming up from the flower petals; 'exstipulata' means not having stipules (appendages growing from the base of the leaf stalk).

Turkey bush

Corymbia bella

Family name: MYRTACEAE (eucalypt family)

Summary: This symbolic Top End ghost gum is often featured on postcards and in photographs. This species differs from its central Australian counterpart by its preference for alluvial soils associated with alluvial flats and drainage areas.

Description: A medium to tall tree to 15 m. The bark is white and smooth and shreds annually. Leaves are mid-green, often with wavy margins, and are linear to lanceolate from 6–16 cm long by 1–5 cm wide. The buds are club-shaped and are up to 1.5 cm long. The flowers are small, creamy white and in groups of 3–6. The cup-shaped fruit are papery and easily crushed between the fingers. These capsules are up to 1.2 cm long and 1 cm wide.

Flowering time: July to November.

Habitat: Grows on levees, alluvial flats, drainage areas and on the margins of alluvial plains.

Distribution: Widespread across northern Australia from Halls Creek, Katherine and the Top End, extending west to Broome and Cape Leveque in Western Australia and east into Queensland.

Origin of name: 'Corymbia' from Greek *corymbos*, a cluster, pertaining to the flowers; 'bella', Latin, *bellus* meaning pretty or beautiful, in reference to the appearance of this species with its white trunk and soft green leafy crowns.

Ghost gum

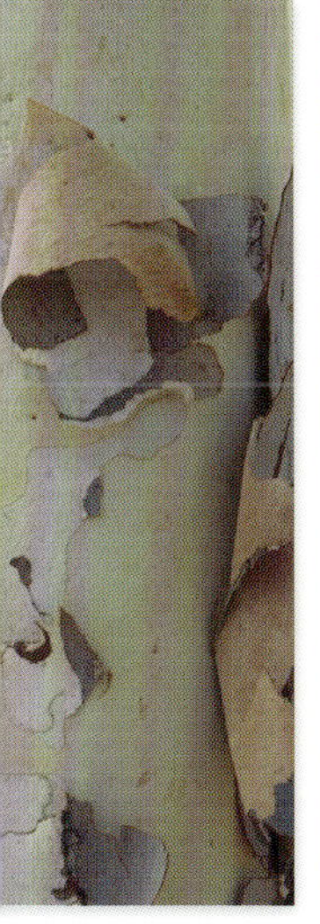

Corymbia polycarpa

Family name: MYRTACEAE (eucalypt family)

Summary: This tall and majestic tree is often overlooked, yet the species is equally as graceful and at home in the Top End as the Darwin woollybutt or Darwin stringybark. The capsules are like small Balinese clay urns, they occur after a profusion of flowering.

Description: A tall tree up to 18 m with a spreading canopy. The bark is grey to brown, rough and tessellated. The leaves are straight or sometimes slightly sickle-shaped, smooth and glossy green above with a paler underside, 7–18 cm long by 1–2.5 cm wide. The large prominent buds are up to 1.5 cm long by 1 cm wide, coarsely coated and in groups of 3–7. These open to reveal large white-cream flowers that are terminally massed in the canopy. The fruit are long and urn-shaped, up to 3 cm long by 1.5 cm wide, and contain numerous red-brown, winged seeds.

Flowering time: March to July.

Habitat: Commonly located on seasonally inundated flats, drainage areas and alluvial plains. Sometimes found on deep sandy soils or sand plains.

Distribution: Widespread in northern Australia, extending to southern Queensland and into northern NSW.

Origin of name: 'polycarpa', Greek *polys* meaning many, and *carpos* fruit, in reference to the many fruit borne by this tree.

Long-fruited bloodwood

Crinum angustifolium

Family name: AMARYLLIDACEAE (daffodil family)

Summary: These lilies herald the wet. After the first decent rains the leaves rise up from perennial bulbs and soon erupt into flower. These bursts of white are scattered along floodplains and low-lying areas. When the dry approaches the leaves wither away, and the plant disappears for another season.

Description: An erect herb to 1 m. The leaves are fleshy, smooth and strap-like and taper to a point. These are mid-green, semi-erect and range from 45–100 cm long by 2–6 cm wide. The flowers are borne on long, fleshy stalks up to 1 m long. The large star-shaped flowers have 6 petals and are white to pale pink with prominent purple/maroon stamens. The fruit are round and light green when ripe and contain several large green seeds.

Flowering time: October to February.

Habitat: Found in wet areas, commonly on floodplains, drainage depressions, creek and mangrove margins, usually in sandy soils.

Distribution: Common across northern Australia, including Western Australia and Queensland.

Origin of name: 'Crinum', Greek *crinon* meaning lily; 'angustifolium', Latin *angusti* narrow, and *folium* leaf, in reference to the tapering of the leaves.

Lily

Cycas armstrongii

Family name: CYCADACEAE (cycad family)

Summary: At their spectacular best re-sprouting after fire or with a new season's growth, these relicts from the past add a mystical beauty to our savannah woodlands. Cycads are a direct link to an ancient world and can best be described as living fossils.

Description: A palm-like plant to 4 m. The bark is dark grey and rough. The leaves are smooth, dark green fronds up to 1 m long and divided into numerous stiff leaflets up to 14 cm long by 0.7 cm wide. The leaves sprout and are clustered at the top of the trunk. New growth is a luminous frog-green. The male plant develops a rusty orange-coloured oval cone, 12–20 cm long, made up of numerous spirally arranged scales. The female plant develops hairy spikes that hang down, with 2–4 spherical fruit attached at the end. The fruit are up to 4 cm in diameter; they are dry, smooth and hard and contain a single seed.

Fruiting time: March to September.

Habitat: Prefers well-drained soils, usually of a lateritic origin in open forests and woodlands.

Distribution: Locally abundant north of Pine Creek and with a small population on Melville Island.

Origin of name: 'Cycas', Greek from *coicas*, doum palm, in reference to the palm-like appearance; 'armstrongii' after John Armstrong (d. 1847), a plant collector for Kew Gardens based at Port Essington (an attempted settlement on Cobourg Peninsula), where he established government gardens.

Cycad

Decaisnina signata

Family name: LORANTHACEAE (mistletoe family)

Summary: The fruit from this woody plant attracts the striking small black and red mistletoe bird. These feed on the berries that are later excreted, largely undigested, onto the branches of other plants where they germinate and take hold. Spread is indiscriminate and is determined by the bird favouring either its natural habitat or a suburban environment.

Description: A semi-parasitic woody plant. The leaves are opposite, smooth, thick and leathery. These vary from lanceolate to elliptic and range from 4–17 cm long by 1.5–6.5 cm wide. The tips are either rounded or pointed and the base is heart-shaped or ends abruptly. The tubular, red flowers are up to 6 cm long in clusters that are arranged one-sided on short stalks. The fruit are orange, fleshy, oval berries up to 1cm long, often with longitudinal stripes, and contain a single sticky seed.

Flowering time: Mainly April to October.

Habitat: Grows on host trees associated with woodland and monsoon forests. In towns or inhabited areas it can be found growing on garden ornamentals.

Distribution: Common in the Top End, extending to the Kimberley and other parts of northern Australia.

Origin of name: 'Decaisnina' after Joseph Decaisne (1807–1882), a French botanist and director of the Paris botanical gardens; 'signata' Latin, *signata* meaning marked, in reference to the stripes on the berries.

Mistletoe

Erythrophleum chlorostachys

Family name: FABACEAE (pea family)

Summary: The wood from these trees is exquisite, but it can be difficult to mill. The wood is particularly hard and dense and also toxic. Most parts of the tree are poisonous; however, brushtail possums and some birds can tolerate the toxicity.

Description: A mostly large and spreading tree to 18 m, occasionally smaller and stunted in shallow skeletal soils. The bark is dark grey to black, rough and tessellated. The leaves are bipinnate, each whole leaf is up to 30 cm long and divided into several paired segments that are further divided into 5–8 leaflets. The flowers are small and creamy white-green on bottle brush–type spikes 5–8 cm long. The fruit are broad and flat and range from 10–20 cm long by 2–4 cm wide. These mature to become brittle and slightly woody pods that contain very hard seeds.

Flowering time: August to November.

Habitat: A widespread species mostly on well-drained soils in open forests, woodlands and sometimes along river levees.

Distribution: Common across northern Australia, including Western Australia and Queensland.

Origin of name: 'Erythrophleum', Greek *erythros* red, and *phloios* bark, in reference to the red sap that flows from cut bark; 'chlorostachys', Greek *chloros* green, and *stachys* ear of corn, flower-spike, in reference to the colour of the flowering spike.

Ironwood

Eucalyptus miniata

Family name: MYRTACEAE (eucalypt family)

Summary: One of the Top End's signature species, these trees bear orange to scarlet flowers and have a distinctive stocking of bark covering the lower trunk. The Darwin woollybutt is a major player in the eucalpyt communities that dominate northern Australia.

Description: A medium to tall tree to 30 m. The bark is dark grey with shreds of orange and red and is rough and fibrous. This stocking is persistent on the lower two thirds of the trunk; the upper bark is smooth and white. Leaves are a glossy mid-green, slightly paler underneath and lanceolate to broadly lanceolate from 8–15 cm by 2–6 cm wide. The buds are pear-shaped and usually ribbed, up to 2.5 cm long by 1.5 cm wide. These develop to produce large orange-red flowers in clusters. The fruit are woody and strongly ribbed, 3-5 cm long by 1-3 cm wide and are formed on short, stout stalks.

Flowering time: May to July (variable depending on the season).

Habitat: A widespread species favouring well-drained soils on plains, slopes and ridges, including sandstone and lateritic country.

Distribution: Widely distributed from north of Larrimah through to the Top End, extending west into the Kimberley region and east across to Burketown and to the base of Cape York.

Origin of name: 'Eucalyptus', Greek *eu* meaning well, and *calyptos* meaning covered, referring to the cap covering the stamens in the bud; 'miniata', Latin, *miniatus* meaning red, in reference to the colour of this species' flowers.

Darwin woollybutt

Eucalyptus phoenicea

Family name: MYRTACEAE (eucalypt family)

Summary: This attractive eucalypt, with its fine foliage and orangey bark, thrives in shallow and skeletal soils. The orange flowers are similar to large powder puffs that develop into equally striking urn-shaped fruit in globular-like arrangements.

Description: An often multi-stemmed, small to medium tree to 12 m. The bark is flaky and fibrous, streaked with grey, orange and yellow on the main trunk, with upper branches redder and smoother. The leaves are a light to mid-green, usually straight and lanceolate in shape, 6.5–14.5 cm long by 1–3.5 cm wide. The buds are club-shaped and arranged globularly from a single point. The flowers are densely packed in these globular arrangements and are pale to dark orange. The fruit are woody, urn-shaped capsules with a distinctive neck and are often slightly ribbed and glossy.

Flowering time: May to August.

Habitat: Found on rocky slopes and plateaux in sandstone country and on granite hills and ridges.

Distribution: Common in the Top End, extending to the Kimberley and parts of Queensland.

Origin of name: 'phoenicea', *phoeniceus*, Latin meaning scarlet-red coloured, in reference to the flowers of this species.

Scarlet gum

Eucalyptus tetrodonta

Family name: MYRTACEAE (eucalypt family)

Summary: The stringybark is another major player in Top End woodland communities. It can form large extensive stands of its own, but is often in association with the Darwin woollybutt, forming one of the most dominant vegetation communities in the Top End.

Description: A medium to tall tree to 30 m. The bark is grey, rough, stringy and fibrous and easily peeled off in longitudinal strips. The leaves are smooth, alternate and sickle shaped. These are a dull dark green, up to 20 cm long by 3 cm wide and have an elongated tip. The buds are club or pear-shaped with 4 prominent points. These mature and open to reveal creamy white flowers, usually in groups of 3. The fruit are cup to bell-shaped, with 4 prominent points around the rim and valves that are either level with or slightly exserted above the rim.

Flowering time: June to October.

Habitat: A widespread species found on a variety of well-drained soils. Usually the tallest and densest populations of stringybark are found on deep, sandy soils.

Distribution: Widely distributed from the Kimberley, to the Top End and across to Cape York.

Origin of name: 'tetrodonta', Greek *tetra* meaning four, and *odous*, *odontos* meaning tooth, in reference to the 4 prominent teeth found on the apex of the buds and fruit.

Darwin stringybark

Eucalyptus tintinnans

Family name: MYRTACEAE (eucalypt family)

Summary: Providing a contrast of colour with its salmon bark, this tree is found in the 'goldfield loop', in the Pine Creek area. The woodland communities containing this species provide a vital habitat for gouldian finches: the hollows of these trees are a nesting refuge for the remaining populations in the Northern Territory.

Description: A semi-deciduous and often multi-branched, small to medium tree to 10 m. The smooth, white and grey bark is shed annually to reveal a new bright orange or salmon layer. The leaves are variable from broadly lanceolate to almost orbicular, 7.5–12.5 cm long by 3.5–7.5 cm wide. The buds are globular, 5–7 mm long by 4–5 mm wide. Small, cream flowers are clustered on short stalks at the end of leaf branchlets. These develop into small, hard, woody capsules with valves that slightly protrude above the rim.

Flowering time: July to August.

Habitat: Grows in shallow, skeletal soils commonly on gravelly hillslopes and rocky ridges of a granitic or sandstone origin.

Distribution: Endemic to the Northern Territory. Locally abundant in the Pine Creek, Mary River and Mount Todd region.

Origin of name: 'tintinnans', Latin *tintinnabulum*, a bell, referring to the hollow trees giving out a ringing, almost musical, note when struck with an axe; the species was originally called ringing gum.

Salmon gum

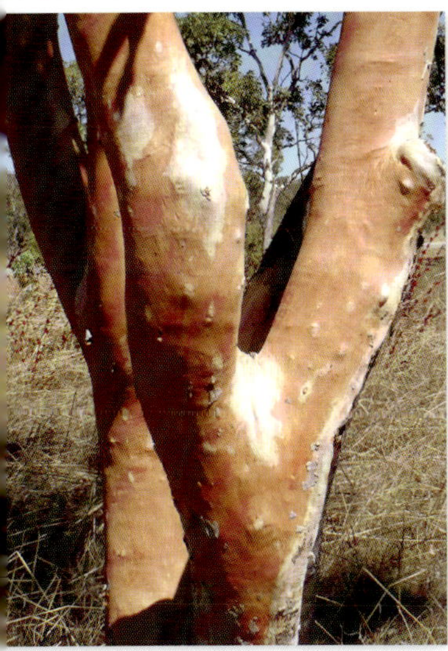

Ficus aculeata

Family name: MORACEAE (fig family)

Summary: The flowers of these trees are hidden inside the figs. Pollination is dependent on small wasps that lay eggs inside the fig to transfer the pollen from the female to male flower. Similarly, the true fruit also develop inside the fig and are reliant on birds and flying foxes for their dispersal and spread.

Description: A shrub or small to medium tree to 8 m. The bark is dark grey, rough and fissured. The leaves are ovate to elliptic, 4–8 cm long by 3–5 cm wide. These are coarse and bristly like sandpaper, with distinct venation, and have a conspicuous pair of veins opposite each other at the base of the leaf. The leaves and stems exude a milky sap when broken. Flowers and true fruit are not seen; instead, these are enclosed in coarse hairy and fleshy figs. The figs are up to 1 cm in diameter and mature to a red-brown when ripe.

Fruiting time: July to February.

Habitat: A widespread understorey species found in open forests, woodlands and shrublands on a variety of soil types.

Distribution: Locally abundant across northern Australia, extends to Western Australia, Queensland, New Guinea and Indonesia.

Origin of name: 'Ficus', the classical Latin name for edible fig; 'aculeata' Latin *aculeata*, furnished with prickles, in reference to the stiff hairs on the figs.

Sandpaper fig

Grevillea dryandri

Family name: PROTEACEAE (grevillea family)

Summary: Gorgeous red flowering sprays and fine, green foliage are a feature of this attractive plant. Widely used in native plantings, it is now commonly seen growing in streetscapes and gardens across the Territory.

Description: A sprawling shrub from 1–2 m. The bark is brown and smooth. The whole leaf is 10–20 cm long and distinctly divided into numerous pairs of slender and narrow lobes. The leaves are green above and silky hairy below. The flowers range from pink to red and occasionally cream or white. These are arranged on spikes to 30 cm borne on prominent branched stalks that protrude up from the foliage. The oval mature fruit are grey to black, thin woody follicles coated in a sticky resin. Each follicle has a persistent style extending from the tip.

Flowering time: March to October.

Habitat: There are two subspecies. The more widespread species is found in open woodlands and shrublands on lateritic soils. The other is associated with sandstone country in the Arnhem Land and Nitmiluk (Katherine Gorge) region.

Distribution: The more common species occurs across the Top End and Kimberley region of Western Australia.

Origin of name: 'Grevillea' in honour of Charles Francis Greville (1749–1809), a founder of the Royal Horticultural Society; 'dryandri' after Jonas Dryander (1748–1810), a Swedish botanist and Sir Joseph Bank's librarian.

Dryander's grevillea

Grevillea pteridifolia

Family name: PROTEACEAE (grevillea family)

Summary: A distinctly recognisable species, this plant stands out with its fern-like foliage and bright orange flowers. The nectar is highly prized by insects, birds, possums, and people. In the horticulture industry the plant is the parent of many of the *Grevillea* hybrids on the market.

Description: A small tree to 8 m. The bark is dark grey, rough and lightly fissured. The fern-like leaves are up to 40 cm long and distinctively divided into narrow lobes up to 18 cm long by 0.4 cm wide; sometimes lower lobes are further divided. The leaves are dark green above and silvery and silky hairy on the underside. The vivid orange flowers are densely grouped on one side of a stalk that is up to 20 cm long. The fruit are oblong semi-woody follicles, 1.5–2 cm long by 1 cm wide with a persistent style at the tip. These split when ripe and contain 2 winged, brown seeds.

Flowering time: May to August.

Habitat: Seasonally wet sandy soils in drainage areas, seepage zones, creek margins and outer fringes of alluvial and floodplains.

Distribution: Widespread in northern Australia.

Origin of name: 'pteridifolia', Greek *pteris*, a type of fern with feathery leaves, and Latin *folium* meaning leaf, in reference to the shape of the leaf.

Fern-leaved grevillea

Hibiscus tiliaceus

Family name: MALVACEAE (hibiscus family)

Summary: This tough and handsome plant can thrive in the most inhospitable conditions. It bears the brunt of harsh coastal environments. It is equally adaptable to growing inland and can tolerate cold winters and frosts.

Description: A many-branched spreading tree to 8 m. The smooth bark is a mottled grey-brown colour. The large, green, heart-shaped leaves have a paler underside and are 8–14 cm by 7–13 cm. The leaves have prominent veins and are sparsely hairy on the surface to densely hairy on the underside. The hibiscus-like flowers are large and yellow with a burgundy centre, 6–7 cm long by 7–9 cm wide. These fade to orange before dropping off and falling to the ground. The fruit develops into a semi-woody, oval capsule that splits on maturity, revealing small, kidney-shaped seeds.

Flowering time: Periodic.

Habitat: Coastal environments including foreshore, sand dunes, vine thickets or cliffs, often in association with mangrove species or in monsoon forest pockets associated with creek lines.

Distribution: Common in coastal habitats across northern Australia, south-east Asia, Africa, India, America and the Pacific Islands.

Origin of name: 'Hibiscus', Greek *hibiscos*, meaning mallow, a reference to the plant type; 'tiliaceus' taken from the plant genus *tillaea*, and *aceus*, a latin suffix meaning 'having the nature of'.

Beach hibiscus

Ipomoea pes-caprae

Family name: CONVOLVULACEAE (morning glory family)

Summary: A beautiful ground cover, this is an important plant for stabilising beach dune habitats and is invaluable in coastal rehabilitation projects. The leaves are used by Aboriginal people to treat stings from catfish, stingrays and spiders.

Description: A perennial vine with trailing stems to 8 m. The leaves are smooth, large and glossy green, oblong to semi-circular and 2-lobed. They are thick and leathery, 4.5–12 cm long by 4–12 cm wide and borne on long stalks to 12 cm long. The flowers are large and bell-shaped, up to 6 cm long and pink to magenta with a darker star-shaped centre. The fruit are smooth, semi-woody, rounded capsules with 4 persistent bracts at the base. These split when mature and contain 4 hairy seeds.

Flowering time: Periodic.

Habitat: Coastal regions, mostly on beach sands and dunes above the high tide mark. Also mangrove fringes and disturbed coastal areas.

Distribution: Widespread across coastal regions of northern Australia and northern NSW. Also occurs in south-east Asia.

Origin of name: 'Ipomoea', Greek *ipos* meaning worm, and *homoios* meaning 'resembling', in reference to the twining habit of this plant; 'pes-caprae' Latin, *pes* foot, and *capra* a goat, in reference to the shape of the leaf (goat's foot).

Beach morning glory

Livistona humilis

Family name: ARECACEAE (palm family)

Summary: An integral part of the Top End woodlands, these small hardy palms are commonly seen in the mid layer. Along with the cycads they add a tropical and Jurassic feel to these old landscapes.

Description: A single-stemmed fan palm to 5 m. The bark is grey and rough with a ringed arrangement. The fan-shaped leaves are dark green, stiff and smooth and are divided to about half way with pointed segments. The leaf stalks are up to 70 cm long, with small sharp spines along the margins. The flowers are arranged on erect and branched spikes to 30 cm long that protrude above the foliage. The flowers are small and yellow, from 0.2–0.4 cm across. The fruit are oval-shaped to 1.5 cm long and mature to a purple-black.

Flowering time: September to May.

Habitat: A common understorey species in open forests and woodlands on sandy or lateritic soils. Occasionally forms dense stands in these habitats.

Distribution: Endemic to the Northern Territory and locally abundant in the Top End.

Origin of name: 'Livistona' after Patrick Murray (d. 1671), Baron of Livingston, who largely established the original Edinburgh botanical garden; 'humilis', Latin, *humilis* meaning low, in reference to the height of the plant.

Sand palm

Melaleuca leucadendra

Family name: MYRTACEAE (eucalypt family)

Summary: Found along creek banks and waterholes, this graceful tree is appreciated by all. The flowers provide a food source for insects, birds and flying foxes. The bark is used by Aboriginal people as a building material for shelters and fish traps, and the leaves are sourced to flavour cooking or for medicinal purposes.

Description: A large and often spreading tree with weeping foliage to 30 m. The bark is white or creamy brown and papery. The leaves are smooth and long, sometimes sickle-shaped and range from 5.5–19 cm long by 0.7–3.7 cm wide. These have 5 or 6 longitudinal veins. The bottle brush flowers are white, cream or greenish-cream on spikes up to 13 cm long by 3 cm wide. The fruit develop on these spikes and are small, brown, woody cup-shaped capsules up to 0.5 cm long by 0.6 cm wide containing numerous seeds.

Flowering time: August to May.

Habitat: Wet habitats such as freshwater creeks, billabongs, seasonally inundated swamps and monsoon vine thickets.

Distribution: Widespread across northern Australia and extending to New Guinea and Malesia.

Origin of name: 'Melaleuca', Greek *melos* black and *leucos* white, in reference to the black bark and white branches of some Asian species; 'leucadendra', Greek *leucos* white, and *dendron* tree, in reference to the white appearance of this tree.

Weeping paperbark

Melaleuca viridiflora

Family name: MYRTACEAE (eucalypt family)

Summary: This small tree is usually an indicator of clay soils in seasonally inundated areas. The species can form extensive stands along floodplain country in the north. Like the weeping paperbark, this tree provides a food source for the native fauna and has a wide number of uses for Aboriginal people.

Description: A small to medium tree to 10 m (occasionally to 16 m). The bark is cream to grey and papery. The dark green leaves are typically broad and thick. These have 5-7 prominent longitudinal veins and range from 7–19 cm long by 2.2–5.5 cm wide. The dense bottle brush–type flowers are green to yellowish green on spikes to 7 cm long. The woody capsules develop on the spikes in dense clusters. These mature to brown, are up to 0.5 cm long by 0.6 cm wide and contain numerous seeds.

Flowering time: February to May.

Habitat: Grows on minor internal drainage channels and creeks, in swamps, lagoons and billabongs. It is also found in clay soils on broad alluvial flats and floodplains or on seasonally wet sandy soils.

Distribution: Widespread across northern Australia, southern Queensland and New Guinea.

Origin of name: 'viridiflora', Latin *viridis* green, and *floris* flower, in reference to the colour of this species' flowers.

Broad-leaved paperbark

Nauclea orientalis

Family name: RUBIACEAE (coffee family)

Summary: A tall, majestic tree commanding a presence alongside its neighbours in creekline habitats. It stands out with its large glossy leaves, lateral branching and sheer size when growing in ideal conditions.

Description: A large deciduous tree to 25 m with horizontal branching. The bark is cream-grey and rough. The leaves are opposite, large, smooth and oval-shaped, 15–30 cm long by 10–18 cm wide. These are a glossy green above and dull on the underside with a distinctive mid-rib and lateral venation. The new leaves and buds are protected by pairs of large, rounded, scale-like stipules. The flowers are yellow with a prominent style and are clustered in dense globular heads up to 5 cm in diameter. The fruit is a globular mass of numerous individual fruit that mature to a yellow-brown when ripe.

Flowering time: August to November.

Habitat: Prefers wet habitats including freshwater creeks, rivers, monsoon vine forests, swamp margins and fringes to clay plains.

Distribution: Common across northern Australia and extending to India and south-east Asia.

Origin of name: 'Nauclea' Greek, *naus* ship, and *cleio* to confine, referring to the boat shape of half the capsule; 'orientalis' Latin, *orientalis* pertaining to the east, in reference to the eastern distribution of this species in relation to other members of the genus.

Leichardt pine

Nelumbo nucifera

Family name: NELUMBONACEAE (lotus lily family)

Summary: Known as the sacred lotus in south-east Asia, this beautiful plant is a feature of our wetlands. It is commonly portrayed on images and postcards of the unique floodplain habitats of the Top End, including those in Kakadu National Park.

Description: A perennial aquatic herb. The leaves are large, circular and blue-green with prominent veins radiating from the centre. The blades are floating or emergent and 18–75 cm in diameter growing from prickly stalks from 0.5–2 m long. The large and distinctive flowers are solitary and borne on erect stems up to 2 m. The flowers have vivid pink petals decreasing in size towards the middle with a prominent yellow centre made up of numerous stamens. The fruit are smooth, hard, nut-like seeds contained loosely in the cavities of a large cone-shaped receptacle from 6–12 cm across. As the receptacle ages, it withers and bends toward the water, releasing the seeds.

Flowering time: March to December.

Habitat: Found on floodplains, swamps and billabongs with permanent water to several meters deep.

Distribution: Locally widespread in the Top End, extends to Queensland, south-east Asia, Thailand, Japan, China and India.

Origin of name: 'Nelumbo' is derived from the Sinhalese word *nelum*; 'nucifera' from *nucifera* meaning nut bearing.

Lotus lily

Nymphaea violacea

Family name: NYMPHAEACEAE (water lily family)

Summary: Fringing billabongs and swamps in a wonderful display of glossy, round lily pads and spectacular flowers, these plants soften the landscape and often lull the senses to the dangers that may lurk beneath the surface of these habitats.

Description: A perennial aquatic herb. The leaves are large, smooth, glossy green and circular. The blades are 10–20 cm in diameter with prominent venation on the underside and with usually wavy margins. The leaves are borne on long fleshy stalks. The large conspicuous flowers are solitary with pink, blue or white petals and numerous yellow stamens in the centre. The flowers are either level with or rise above the water on long, erect stems. The fruit are spongy globular to urn-shaped green berries to 5 cm wide and hold numerous seeds.

Flowering time: Periodic, generally January to July.

Habitat: Common in seasonally inundated freshwater swamps, billabongs, brackish creeks and drainage lines.

Distribution: Widespread in the Top End and extending to Western Australia, Queensland and New Guinea.

Origin of name: 'Nymphaea', Latin, *nymphaea* meaning water nymphs, in reference to the plant being a water lily; 'violacea', Latin *viola*, referring to the colour of the flowers.

Water lily

Nymphoides indica

Family name: MENYANTHACEAE (snowflake lily family)

Summary: Carpeting lagoons and billabongs in a layer of green with delicately fringed white flowers, this aquatic plant is an image to behold. These displays can last long into the dry season. Although the species may look soft, this is a robust and hardy aquatic plant.

Description: An annual or perennial aquatic herb. The leaves are thick, smooth, glossy green and heart-shaped, 2–27 cm long by 2–25 cm wide. These are attached to long, slender stems rising from the submerged base. The flowers are white, with distinctly fringed petals and a yellow or orange throat. These are usually solitary, rising from clusters of stalks, 2–8 cm long, and grow up from stems below the base of the leaf. The fruit are small, globular to oval-shaped capsules to 0.8 cm long and contain numerous smooth or rough, globular, pale brown to dark grey seeds.

Flowering time: February to October.

Habitat: Found in seasonally wet or permanent swamps, drainage areas, wetlands, and creeks. Grows in a variety of soils.

Distribution: Widespread in northern Northern Territory, including areas south of Tennant Creek. Also occurs in Western Australia, Queensland and northern NSW. A widespread pan-tropical species.

Origin of name: 'Nymphoides', Greek, *nymphoides* pertaining to a demi-goddess inhabiting springs and rivers, in reference to the plant's habitat; 'indica', Latin, *indica* pertaining to India or the Far East, in reference to the distribution of this species.

White snowflake lily

Pandanus spiralis

Family name: PANDANACEAE (pandan family)

Summary: You know you're in the Top End when you see these trees. Standing tall like Dr Seuss plants, pandanus inhabit the drainage depressions and alluvial plains across the north. The leaves from this plant are widely used by Aboriginal women to make their famous dilly bags, mats and baskets.

Description: An often multi-branched tree to 10 m. The trunk is grey, rough and fibrous with spirally arranged leaf scars. The leaves sit tuft-like at the top of the trunk. Each strap-like leaf is up to 2 m long with small spines along the margins and midrib. There are separate male and female plants, both with small, white flowers. The female plant bears large pineapple-like fruit up to 20 cm across. These are made up of many individual woody wedge-shaped segments, 5–7 cm by 4–10 cm, that contain the seeds. The fruit matures to a vivid orange-red before dropping to the ground.

Fruiting time: June to October.

Habitat: Favours poorly drained soils in drainage depressions, alluvial plains, floodplain margins and creeks. It is also an understorey tree in open forest and woodlands and along coastal habitats in reasonably well-drained sandy or earthy soils.

Distribution: Widespread across northern Australia.

Origin of name: 'Pandanus' from *pandan*, the Malayan name for these plants; 'spiralis', Latin, *spiralis* meaning spirally coiled, in reference to the leaf arrangement.

Pandanus

Planchonia careya

Family name: LECYTHIDACEAE (brazil nut family)

Summary: The large flowers of this rather untidy little tree are striking, and its leaves turn a wine-red in the late dry season. It has been used by Aboriginal people for the treatment of wounds. Research has validated its use as a healing remedy by isolating antibacterial compounds in the leaves of this plant.

Description: A straggly, semi-deciduous, small to medium tree to 10 m. The bark is grey, rough and corky. The leaves are light green and oval-shaped, 4–10 cm long by 3–6 cm wide. These have slightly serrated margins and during the dry season change to a red-pink. The flowers are large and showy, with 4 white petals at the base with numerous creamy and pink stamens to 6 cm long. The fruit are fleshly and oblong to pear-shaped. The pear-shaped fruit ripen to a pale green, and are up to 10 cm long by 3.7 cm wide.

Flowering time: July to October.

Habitat: A common understorey tree in open forests and woodlands on a range of well-drained soils.

Distribution: Common across the Top End, extends to the Victoria River District, Western Australia, Queensland and New Guinea.

Origin of name: 'Planchonia', after Jules Emile Planchon (1823–1888), a French botanist responsible for plant collections at Kew Gardens, later director of Montpellier botanical gardens, who introduced eucalypts to France; 'careya', after William Carey (1761–1834), botanist and professor in India and editor of Roxburgh's *Flora Indica.*

Cocky apple

Sorghum intrans

Family name: POACEAE (grass family)

Summary: When these plants are well into their growing season you can bet on the weather being hot and sticky. They are at their tallest and greenest midway through the wet season. By the time they flower and begin to hay off they are vulnerable to the 'knock-'em' down rains that come at the end of the Wet, when these tall grasses can be flattened by the last mad, sporadic and heavy downpours.

Description: A large, erect annual grass to 3.5 m. The leaves are long, flat and narrow with blades to 1.5 cm wide on tall robust stems. The flowers are small and inconspicuous. The seeds develop on long and densely grouped seed heads. These mature to brown, are up to 40 cm long and stand high above the plant. Each seed is spear-shaped with a prominent and beak-like hairy point at the tip and a long bristle at the top. The seeds are golden and the hairs and bristles are rusty red-brown.

Flowering time: January to April.

Habitat: Grows in open and sparse woodlands on a variety of soil types with a lateritic or granitic origin. Commonly found on plains, rises, hills and drainage lines.

Distribution: Confined to the north-west of the Northern Territory. Widespread in the Top End.

Origin of name: 'Sorghum', Italian *sorgho*, the name for these plants; 'intrans', Latin *intrans* meaning piercing, in reference to the self-burying ability of the seeds.

Spear grass

Sterculia quadrifida

Family name: MALVACEAE (hibiscus family)

Summary: With its stunning orange-red, boat-like fruit encasing edible nuts, the peanut tree really catches your eye. The tree tends to lose its distinct dark green, heart-shaped leaves when fruiting during the dry season, which adds to the effect. Its roots and trunk are known to house witchetty grubs.

Description: A deciduous tree to 15 m. The bark is grey and smooth. The leaves are large and broadly ovate to heart-shaped, 10–18 cm long by 6–7 cm wide. These are smooth above and finely hairy on the underside with leaf stalks from 4–10 cm long. The flowers are green-yellow to 5 mm long with 4 petals and loosely clustered on short stalks at the end of branches. The distinctive fruit are oval shaped, smooth and leathery, maturing to orange or scarlet. These are 4–7 cm long by 2–3 cm wide and split to reveal up to 5, sometimes more, glossy black oblong seeds.

Flowering time: February to November.

Habitat: Grows in semi-deciduous, coastal monsoon vine forests and thickets and occasionally in open forests or woodlands fringing drainage areas.

Distribution: Locally abundant in the Top End and extending to Western Australia, Queensland, NSW and New Guinea.

Origin of name: 'Sterculia' from Sterculius, a Roman god of dung and privies, in reference to the bad smell of flowers from some species in this genus; 'quadrifida', Latin *quadrifida* meaning split into four parts, in reference the four-petalled flower.

Peanut tree

Syzygium suborbiculare

Family name: MYRTACEAE (eucalypt family)

Summary: Arguably the most attractive of all the *Syzygium* species in the Top End. The large, glossy leaves of this well balanced tree are offset by sizeable and showy white flowers and later in the season by the glossy red apple-like fruit.

Description: A rounded medium tree to 12 m, rarely taller. The bark is grey and smooth to slightly rough. The large opposite thick and leathery leaves are oval to almost circular, 9–17 cm long by 7–12 cm wide. These are glossy green above with a paler underside and conspicuous venation. The distinctive flowers are large and white with numerous protruding stamens to 5 cm. These are in dense terminal clusters. The large fruit are fleshy and globular, 5–7 cm long by 4–8 cm wide, ribbed with a persistent calyx at the base. The fruit matures to a deep red when ripe.

Flowering time: July to October.

Habitat: Common understorey tree in open forests, woodlands, monsoon vine forests and coastal floodplain margins. Favours well-drained soils.

Distribution: Common across northern Australia and New Guinea.

Origin of name: 'Syzygium', Greek *syzygia* meaning union, in reference to the fused outer petals; 'suborbiculare', Latin *suborbiculare*, somewhat rounded, in reference to the leaf shape.

Red bush apple

Terminalia ferdinandiana

Family name: COMBRETACEAE (terminalia family)

Summary: The fruit from this tree is a super food: it has the highest level of vitamin C of any natural product anywhere in the world. It is recognised globally as having enormous product potential as a gourmet food item and an ingredient for the health and beauty and pharmaceutical industries.

Description: A deciduous, small to medium spreading tree to 8 m. The bark is grey and tessellated, sometimes irregularly so. Leaves are spirally arranged on stalks 2–10 cm long and crowded towards the end of branches. The leaves are broadly elliptical to circular, 5–25 cm long by 5–25 cm wide, with small hollows present along the mid vein, and occasionally sparsely hairy. The small, cream flowers are borne on long, narrow spikes up to 25 cm. The fruit are oval-shaped and mature to fleshy yellow-green dupes up to 1.5–2.5 cm long by 1–2 cm wide and have a short beak.

Flowering time: October to December.

Habitat: An understorey tree in open eucalypt forests and woodlands on well-drained soils. Occasionally found on rocky sites or as stunted forms after frequent fires.

Distribution: Common in the Top End and extending to the Kimberley region.

Origin of name: 'Terminalia', Latin *terminalis* pertaining to boundaries, in reference to the leaves, bunched at end of branches; 'ferdinandiana' after Sir Ferdinand Mueller (1825–1896), a famous botanist responsible for plant exploration in the Top End.

Billy goat plum

Botanical name index